GEOFINITY

An Adventure in Geometry for Primary Kids

By
Joan Brownlee
Chris Miller
and
Lyndy VanHoutan

Pieces of Learning

© 2003 Pieces of Learning
CLC0307
ISBN 1-931334-26-9
www.piecesoflearning.com
Printed in the U.S.A.

Table of Contents

Introduction

Who needs this book?

Geofinity is written for young mathematicians and their teachers. It is designed to make math enrichment fun for the student and easy for you, whether you are a regular classroom teacher, enrichment coordinator, or teacher of the Gifted and Talented.

Each activity in this book is designed for hands-on math inquiry. Each is written to be developmentally appropriate yet challenging, and done with commonly available materials and minimal preparation. The activities support the NCTM standards for the strands of Geometry, Measurement, Problem Solving, and Connections. (See page 9).

Contents

This book contains two Curriculum Contract Challenge Units (CCCU). Level One is designed for grades 1 through 3 and offers individual lessons in the language of geometry and definitions of shapes, angles, and coordinates. Level Two is for grades 2 through 4, and offers additional lessons in parallel and perpendicular line segments and perimeter. Level Two also offers a more detailed series of lessons in the vocabulary and definition of angles and polygons. Both levels include language arts objectives.

The activities are designed to be done independently by students but may be used in small group sessions. These units are ideal for providing differentiation to a variety of levels of students in your class. We suggest that you give students a pretest to see if they would benefit from the mathematical concepts and additional enrichment presented in this unit. The Geofinity unit extends the curriculum, while still reinforcing state and national standards.

Background on Triple "C" Units (Brownlee, Miller, VanHoutan)

The *Curriculum Contract Challenge* Units were developed by the authors as independent study units directed by a contract. Topics integrate content areas, are based on student interest, offer student choice, and challenge students with real-world problems. Each contract has objectives that are aligned to national curriculum standards.

Research shows that high ability learners need curriculum that . . .

- Allows depth and breadth of inquiry
- Encourages interest-based learning
- Includes real-world problems
- Offers an individualized pace
- Presents choices
- Demands metacognition

Suggestions for Classroom Use

A Triple "C" unit only needs a corner of your desktop or a small space on a bookshelf. Using a cardboard file caddy box, available at most office supply stores (see resources), you can literally offer your students a buffet of learning on a small bookshelf!

Organizing Geofinity

Careful organization of the unit materials and an understanding of the contract format will insure your students' independence.

File Box Organization

- Begin with a colorful box labeled with the unit's name.
- Make several copies of the contract and any activity sheets or papers. Group these in separate file folders.
- Place copies of the contract in a folder at the front of your file box.
- Label the other folders to match the BOLD titles on the contract.
- Arrange folders in the unit box according to the contract.

Contract Format

Student Name – Signing a contract indicates an agreement to complete all of the work.

Title on Student Contract – Centered on top for easy identification.

Activities – Listed in order of expected completion.

Folder Titles - Written in **BOLD**

Extra Resources – (Such as books or videos) Underlined in *ITALICS*

The Grande Finale – The culminating activity in which students demonstrate what they have learned through this contract. Often this includes a choice as to what the project involves and/or how it is presented.

Rubric – A rubric for evaluating the project is included for the student. This information clarifies expectations for the project before the student begins.

Level Two
Place all of the material for Level Two behind Level One.

The Daily Plan Sheet

Ask the students to complete a Daily Plan Sheet each time they work in Geofinity. This encourages metacognition, and it also ensures communication and support from the teacher. A sample plan sheet is on page 8.

A Word about Classroom Management

Students can become so motivated and excited about their work when doing a Triple "C" unit, it may be difficult to get them to stop their independent study and return to whole class work.

To encourage a positive, yet structured, learning environment for independent learners, we recommend clear rules and conditions for students to follow. Teaching Gifted Kids in the Regular Classroom has an excellent example of a Working Conditions Contract to set the climate for independent work.

Resources

Burns, Marilyn. <u>The Greedy Triangle</u>. New York: Scholastic, Inc., 1995.

MacCarone, Grace. <u>Goldie Locks and the Three Squares</u>. New York: Scholastic, Inc., 1996.

Winebrenner, Susan. <u>Teaching Gifted Kids in the Regular Classroom</u>. Minneapolis: Free Spirit Publishing, 2001.

Organizing Tools

A wide variety of colorful file caddies are available through:
>
> Calloway House
> 451 Richardson Drive
> Lancaster, PA 17603-4098
> (1-800-233-0290)

Handy Web Sites

- <u>http://www.amazon.com</u> (great for books and supplies)

- <u>http://www.barnesandnoble.com</u> (great for books and supplies)

- <u>http://www.edstandards.org</u> (A terrific site for locating national standards by state, subject area, government agency, etc.

PLAN SHEET

NAME _____

DATE _____

CENTER _____

TODAY IN MY CENTER I PLAN

_____

_____

_____

TODAY, I

_____

_____

_____

_____

NEXT TIME I

WILL_____

_____

_____

_____

MY TEACHER'S REFLECTIONS

_____

_____

National Standards*

In Geofinity Level One and Level Two the student will . . .

GEOMETRY
- Analyze characteristics and properties of two- and three-dimensional geometric shapes and develop mathematical arguments about geometric relationships.
- Specify locations and describe spatial relationships using coordinate geometry and other representational systems.
- Apply transformations and use symmetry to analyze mathematical situations.
- Use visualization, spatial reasoning, and modeling to solve problems.

MEASUREMENT
- Understand measurable attributes of objects and the units, systems, and processes of measurement.
- Apply appropriate techniques, tools, and formulas to determine measurements.

PROBLEM SOLVING
- Build new mathematical knowledge through problem solving.
- Solve problems that arise in mathematics and other contexts.
- Apply and adapt a variety of strategies to solve problems.
- Monitor and reflect on the process of mathematical problem solving.

CONNECTIONS
- Recognize and use connections among mathematical ideas.
- Understand how mathematical ideas interconnect and build on one another to produce a coherent whole.
- Recognize and apply mathematics in contexts outside of mathematics.

* From <u>Principles and Standards for School Mathematics</u>, Chapter 5, "Standards for Grades 3-5" http://standards.nctm.org

State Standards
Level 1 Contract

California Standards	Texas Essential Knowledge and Skills	Virginia Standards of Learning	Your State
Math: Measurement & Geometry 1.2.1 Students will identify, describe and compare triangles, rectangles, squares, and circles, including faces of three-dimensional objects. **Math: Measurement & Geometry 3.2.0** Students will describe and compare the attributes of plane and solid geometric figures.	**Math 1.6.A** Students will use attributes to identify, compare, and contrast shapes and solids using informal language. **Math 2.7.A, B** Students will use attributes to identify, compare, and contrast shapes and solids.	**Math 1.16** Students will draw and describe triangles, squares, rectangles, and circles according to number of sides, corners, and square corners. **Math 6.14** Students will recognize and create basic shapes and figures.	
Math: Measurement & Geometry K.2.0 Students will identify common objects in their environment and describe geometric figures.	**Math K.9.B** Students will recognize characteristics of shapes in real-life objects or solids.	**Math 1.17** Students will identify and describe objects in his/her environment that depict geometric figures: triangle, rectangle, square, and circle.	
Math: Measurement & Geometry 1.2.2 Students will classify familiar plane and solid objects by common attributes, such as shape, or number of corners, and explain which attributes are being used for classification. **Math: Measurement & Geometry 3.2.0** Students will describe and compare the attributes of plane and solid geometric figures.	**Math 4.8.C** Students will name, describe and compare shapes and solids in terms of vertices, edges, and faces.	**Math 3.18** Students will analyze plane and solid geometric figures and identify relevant properties, including the number of corners, square corners, the shape of faces, and edges. **Math 6.14** Students will recognize and create basic shapes and figures.	
Math: Measurement & Geometry 3.2.4 Students will identify right angles in geometric figures or in appropriate objects and determine whether angles are greater than or less than a right angle. **4.3.5** Students will know the definitions of a right, an acute, and an obtuse angle.	**Math 4.8.A, C** Students will identify and describe lines, shapes and solids using formal geometric language to include right, acute, and obtuse angles, and to describe shapes and solids in terms of vertices, edges, and faces.	**Math 3.19, 4.16** Students will identify and draw representations of line segments, and angles, using a ruler or a straight edge. **Math 5.13** Students will classify angles as right, obtuse, or acute.	
Math: Measurement & Geometry 4.2.0 Students will use two dimensional coordinate grids to represent points.	**Math 5.9** Students will recognize the connection between ordered pairs of numbers and location of points on a plane.	**Math 5.15** Students will identify the ordered pair for a point and locate the point for an ordered pair in the first quadrant of a coordinate plane.	
Language Arts 3.2.6 Students will extract appropriate and significant information from the text.	**English Language Arts 2.7, 3.7** Students will read widely for different purposes in varied sources.	**English 2.7, 3.6** Students will read fiction, nonfiction, and poetry using a variety of strategies independently.	
Language Arts 3.3.0 Students will read and respond to a wide variety of significant works of children's literature.	**English Language Arts 1.13, 2.10** Students will respond to various texts.	**English 3.5** Students will demonstrate comprehension of a variety of written material.	

State Standards

Level 2 Contract

California Standards	Texas Essential Knowledge and Skills	Virginia Standards of Learning	Your State
Math: Measurement & Geometry **2.1.3** Students will measure the length of an object to the nearest inch or centimeter. **3.1.3** Students will find the perimeter of a polygon with integer sides.	**Math 3.11.B** Students will select and use appropriate units of linear measure to find the perimeter of a shape.	**Math 2.12, 4.14** Students will estimate and then use a ruler to make linear measurements to the nearest centimeter and inch, including the distance around a polygon (determine perimeter).	
Math: Measurement & Geometry **2.2.1** Students will describe and classify plane and solid geometric shapes according to the number of and shape of faces, edges, and vertices.	**Math 4.8.C** Students will name, describe and compare shapes and solids in terms of vertices, edges, and faces.	**Math 3.18** Students will analyze plane and solid geometric figures and identify relevant properties, including the number of corners, square corners, the shape of faces and edges.	
Math: Measurement & Geometry **3.2.4** Students will identify right angles in geometric figures or in appropriate objects and determine whether other angles are greater than or less than a right angle.	**Math 4.8** Students will identify and describe lines, shapes and solids using formal geometric language.	**Math 3.19** Students will identify and draw representations of line segments, and angles, using a ruler or a straight edge.	
Writing 3.3.0 Students will write and speak with a command of standard English conventions. **Writing 3.2.2** Students will write descriptive narratives that use concrete sensory details to represent and support unified impressions of people, places, things, or experiences.	**English Language Arts 2.18** Students will select and use writing processes for self initiated and assigned writings.	**English 2.10, 3.8** Students will edit final writing for grammar, capitalization, punctuation, and spelling. **English 3.7** Students will write descriptive paragraphs.	
Writing 3.2.0 Students will write compositions that describe and explain familiar objects, events, and experiences to include: narratives, descriptions, and letters.	**English Language Arts 3.14** Students will write for a variety of audiences and purposes and in various forms.	**English 3.8** Students will write stories, letters, simple explanations, and short reports across all content areas.	

Materials List For Geofinity
Level One

Geo Language Activity
- 1 box of flat toothpicks
- Sheets of plain, unlined white paper
- Glue – white
- Scissors
- Pencil, markers, or crayons
- Definition sheet (provided in unit)

Build a Spaceship Activity
- One bag of tangram shapes (complete set of 7)
- Light-colored crayons
- Attribute Blocks (optional)

Meet the Aliens
- Light-colored or white construction paper
- Bag of "face shapes" (large obtuse, right, and acute angles made from "wonder foam" or cardboard—one each. Templates provided in the unit)
- Bag of plastic eyes (purchase from craft store or catalog)
- Glue
- Crayons or pencils

Angle School
- Angle worksheet (provided in contract unit)
- Protractors
- Plastic strips attached at ends by brads (*Geostrips* from Cuisenaire) or 4" cardboard strips with holes on each end; brad fasteners to use during teacher "mini lesson" about angles

Geo School
- Geo school star chart packet (provided in contract unit)

Heading Back Home (#6 on level one contract)
- Spaceship student already made in activity #2 (Build a Spaceship)
- Geolanguage Guidebook from Geolanguage Activity (for student reference)

Grande Finale
- Book – *Goldie Locks and the Three Squares*- by Grace Maccarone (ISBN 0-590-54344-X) published by Scholastic Inc.
- White construction paper
- Lined notebook paper
- Geoboard dot paper (template provided in unit)

Materials List For Geofinity
Level Two

Dictionary of Spatial Terms
- Definition sheet (provided in contract unit)
- Sheets of white paper or 14-"3x5" cards
- Glue
- Scissors
- Pencil, markers, or crayons
- Ruler

Ship Shape
- Activity sheet (provided in contract unit)

Parallel and Perpendicular Lines
- Parallel and perpendicular lines activity sheet (provided in contract unit)

Polygon Planets
- Polygon Planets activity (provided in contract unit)
- Crayons and pencil

Geo-Class
- Geo-Class packet (provided in contract unit)
- Geoboard and rubber bands (order from math catalog)

Perimeter
- Geoboard and rubber bands
- Perimeter packet about alien civilizations (provided in contract unit)

Scope Out Some Angles
- Scope Out Some Angles activity (provided in contract unit)

Grande Finale
- *The Greedy Triangle* book by Marilyn Burns, published by Scholastic Inc. ISBN 0-590-48991-7
- Geoboard recording paper (provided in contract unit)
- Notebook paper and plain white paper for illustrations
- Geoboard and rubber bands

Teacher Notes for Level One

Before starting Level One of <u>Geofinity</u>, you may want to have a mini-lesson with your students about **degrees** and angles and how to use a **protractor**. Even very young children (first and second grade) enjoy this lesson and understand the concept of an "**angle**" much better after this discussion.

Suggested materials for introductory lesson:

1. Clear protractors
2. Overhead projector
3. Plastic **Geostrips** with holes on the ends, one for each child and one for the teacher (ETA Cuisenaire Geostrips Kit) OR straight 4 inch strips made from poster board
4. Metal brads to attach two plastic or cardboard strips together on ends (Students will rotate the ends to form different angles.)

Allow students to make right, acute, and obtuse angles with their Geostrips and bring them up to the overhead to measure with the large protractor.

Use the plastic **Geostrips** attached with brads in later lessons as the children begin their journey to Planet Geo and also attend Angle School.

GEOFINITY
LEVEL 1 CONTRACT

NAME _____

DATE _____

WELCOME TO A GEOMETRY ADVENTURE!! You have been selected to take a trip to a new planet called Geo. As you begin your trip, you will learn about shapes. Once you get to planet Geo, you will meet some aliens. Let's get ready!

_____ 1. Before we begin our trip to Planet Geo, you will need to complete the **Geolanguage** Activity to help you learn the important words that are spoken on Planet Geo. (Look for a folder in the Geofinity box by this title.)

_____ 2. You are now ready to go on your trip to Planet Geo. But Wait! You will need to **Build a Spaceship** for your travels! (Look for a folder by this title.)

_____ 3. Welcome to Planet Geo! Your spaceship brought you safely to the planet. It is time for you to **Meet the Aliens** and use some of your Geolanguage on this planet. (Look for a folder of instructions by this name.)

_____ 4. You made some new alien friends and they want you to go with them to **Angle School**. (Look for a folder by this title.)

_____ 5. Wow, you did well in Angle School! Now you are invited to go with the aliens to **Geo School** to learn how to make star charts. (Look for a folder by this title.)

_____ 6. Now that your star charts are completed, it is almost time for you to go back home. Your alien teacher tells you that your spaceship needs many different angles so that it can guide you through your star charts.

- Get out the spaceship that you already built in Activity 2, and your Geolanguage guidebook.
- To program your spaceship, label all the different kinds of angles on your ship.
  - o Draw lines that point to some of the <u>acute</u> angles on your ship. Label each of these angles "A" for acute angle.
  - o Draw lines that point to some <u>right</u> angles – label them "R".
  - o Draw lines that point to some <u>obtuse</u> angles – label them "O".

The Grande Finale

You made it back home safely! What a great astronaut you are! ☺

Everyone back home wants to hear all about your space adventure!

_____ Find the folder labeled **Grande Finale** and **read** through all of the directions on the Grande Finale contract.

_____ **Read** the **rubric** (grading chart) at the end of the contract and find out how you can get a good score.

_____ Read the book *Goldie Locks and the Three Squares*. It is about someone who also had a shape adventure like you.

_____ Finish the Grande Finale Contract and complete the **rubric** at the end.

Geolanguage Activity

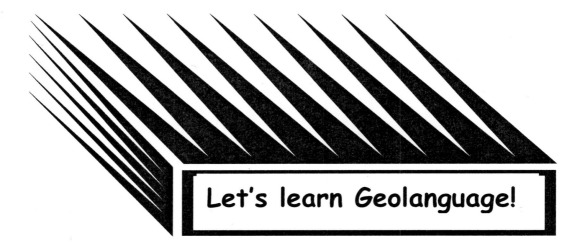

Let's learn Geolanguage!

1. Gather the following materials so that you can make a Geolanguage guide book:

   - 7 blank sheets of unlined, white paper
   - 1 large sheet of construction paper
   - Glue, scissors, pencil, markers or crayons
   - Flat toothpicks, at least 35
   - **Definitions in Geometry** sheet
   - Protractor or plastic *Geostrips* attached with a brad

2. First get <u>7 sheets of plain white paper</u> and a <u>large sheet of construction paper</u>.

   - Fold the construction paper in half.

- Cut out the <u>title</u> on the **Definitions in Geometry** sheet. Glue it at the top of the front page of the construction paper cover.

- Decorate the cover with things that remind you of a trip in space. Put your name at the <u>bottom</u> of the cover. Set the cover aside. You will use it later.

3. On the <u>top</u> of each white sheet, glue a **definition**. Cut out one definition at a time from your **Definitions in Geometry** sheet.
    a. At the <u>bottom</u> of the page, arrange toothpicks on the paper to form the correct shape that goes with the definition.
    b. Glue in place by dipping <u>each end</u> of the toothpick in glue and then pressing the toothpick on the paper.
    c. Complete one new page for each definition on your activity sheet.

4. After the pages have dried, put them all inside the construction paper cover. Have your teacher help you staple the book together. Make sure that the title is on the front page of your booklet!

Definitions in Geometry
Geolanguage

Square
A flat figure with
four equal sides and
four right angles.

Rectangle
Any flat figure with four
right angles and four sides.

Note: When you use toothpicks to
make a rectangle, start with six of
them.

Triangle
A flat figure with three
sides and three angles.

Right Triangle
A triangle with a right
angle, or a 90-degree angle.

Note: When you use toothpicks to
make this shape, you will have to break
one toothpick in half.

Definitions in Geometry

Angle
The shape made by two straight lines meeting in a point.

Acute Angle
An angle that is less than a right angle.
(The angle could look something like this.)

This is an angle formed that is <u>less than</u> 90 degrees.

Obtuse Angle
An angle that is bigger than a right angle.
(The angle could look something like this.)

The angle formed is <u>greater than</u> 90 degrees.

Right Angle
An angle that is formed when two lines meet and form an "L."

Build a Spaceship

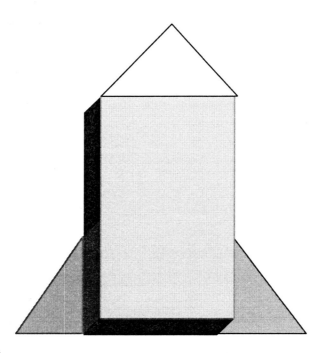

Directions

1. Use a set of Tangrams or Attribute Blocks for this activity. Place them on a piece of plain, light-colored or white paper.

2. Make your own spaceship design from the shapes.

- Hold each shape down carefully and trace all the way around each shape with your pencil.
- Pick the shapes up and you will see the spaceship you made!

3. Using a <u>light</u> colored crayon, color in your spaceship. Make sure that you can still see all the lines that are between each shape!

Meet the Aliens

**Oh COOL! Look at these aliens from Planet Geo!
They have angles on their bodies and special eyes
so they can see everywhere!**

1. If you want to meet more friends, you will have to
    make them. Here is how you will make three new
    friends.

    ▪ Get a piece of light-colored or white construction
    paper. Write your name on the BOTTOM CORNER of
    the paper.

    ▪ Take the bag that is labeled FACE SHAPES out of
    the Geofinity box and place the shapes on your table.
    Choose one shape out of the bag. This shape is actually
    going to become the face of an alien!

    ▪ Place this shape AT THE TOP OF one of your pieces
    of construction paper. Trace around all of the sides to
    form your alien's angle-shaped face on the
    construction paper.

- With your pencil, make a dotted line on your construction paper face just like you see on the foam/cardboard shape. This is where you will glue on the alien's eyes.

- Take a bottle of white glue and put a line of glue on this dotted line on the construction paper. (Do not put the glue on the foam/cardboard shape!)

- Find the bag of plastic eyes in the Geofinity box. Glue a row of plastic eyes from the bag to the dotted line of glue that you just made on your angle alien "face." Place from one to four eyes on your alien's face. (The line of glue will dry soon and will make the alien look awesome.)

- Now add details to your alien. Take a crayon and draw a body, arms and legs so that your alien will be able to walk and carry things.

- Decide if his face is a RIGHT angle, ACUTE angle, or OBTUSE angle. Write the correct NAME (Right, Acute, or Obtuse) under the Alien's picture and set it aside to dry.

2. Now, REPEAT THE STEPS above for the other two angle faces. Put your name on TWO new sheets of construction paper. Make the other two aliens and write their names below their faces on each paper.

NOW YOU HAVE THREE NEW ALIEN FRIENDS. GOOD JOB!

Alien Face Shape Templates

ACUTE ANGLE

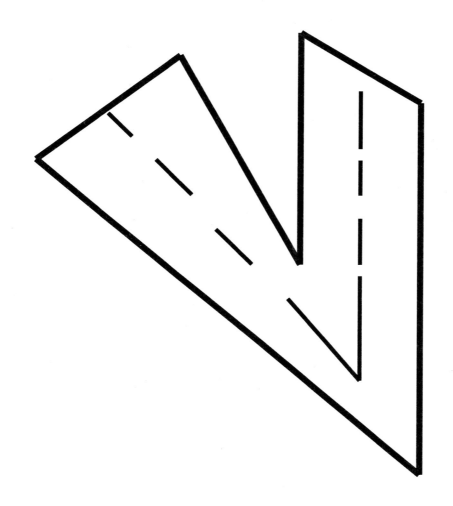

OBTUSE ANGLE

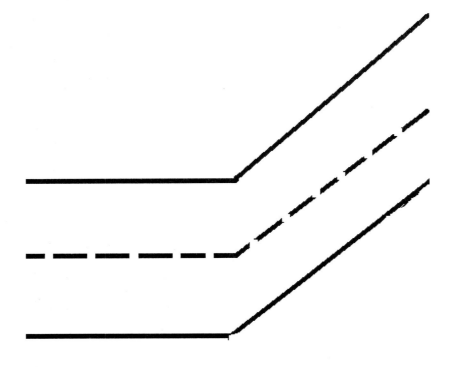

RIGHT ANGLE

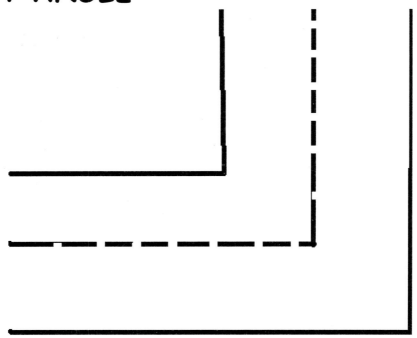

Angle School

The aliens insist that you know your angles. Look at these shapes. Do you see any angles inside? Place an **X** on <u>each</u> ANGLE you see.

1.

2.

3.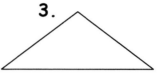

4.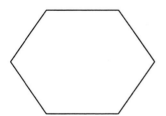

5.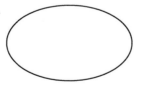

6.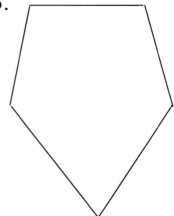

Now find the RIGHT angles. Place an X on <u>each</u> RIGHT ANGLE! (Some shapes may not have any!)

7. 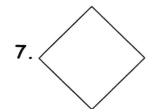   8. 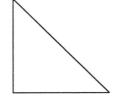   9.

Now find the ACUTE angles. Place an X on <u>each</u> ACUTE ANGLE!

10. 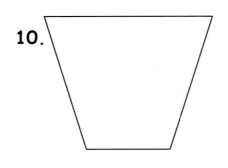   11. 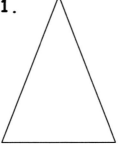   12.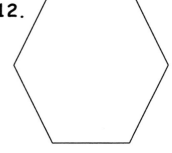

Finally, find the OBTUSE angles. Place an X on <u>each</u> OBTUSE ANGLE.

13. 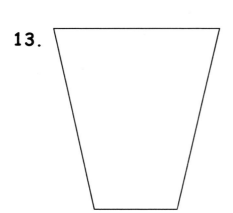   14. 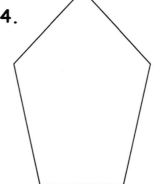   15.

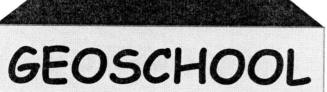

GEOSCHOOL

GEOSCHOOL

Star Charts
FIND THE PLANETS

Let's learn about coordinates in space!

You have gone on a field trip to the observatory. Here you will learn Planet Geo Navigation and make a star chart to get you home.

- Look at the Geo Star Chart below.
- Each planet is marked with a square, a diamond, an octagon, or a star.
- Find the location by telling how many places it is from the left side and the bottom. These locations are your planet coordinates.

GEO STAR CHART ONE

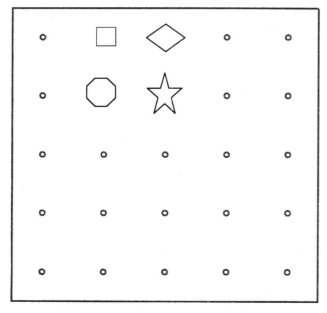

PLANET ☐ IS _2_ FROM THE LEFT SIDE __5__ FROM THE BOTTOM OF THE GRID.

PLANET ◇ IS ____FROM THE LEFT AND____ FROM THE BOTTOM OF THE GRID.

PLANET ⬡ IS ____ FROM THE LEFT AND____ FROM THE BOTTOM OF THE GRID.

PLANET ☆ IS ____ FROM THE LEFT AND ____ FROM THE BOTTOM OF THE GRID.

GEO STAR CHART TWO

Now practice making Star Charts on your geoboard.

- Make each constellation in the correct location on your geoboard.
- Count the total number of pins the rubber band touches.

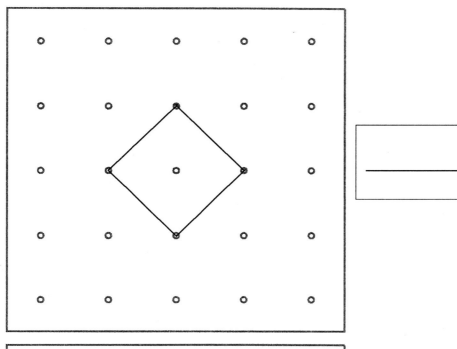

_____ PINS

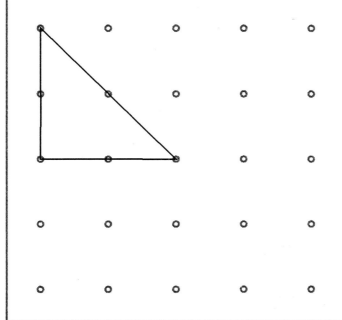

_____ PINS

GEO STAR CHART THREE

Make each constellation on your geoboard.
Count the total number of pins the rubber
band touches. Put an "**x**" on <u>each</u> acute angle
in the figures below.

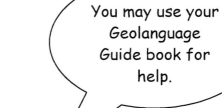

You may use your
Geolanguage
Guide book for
help.

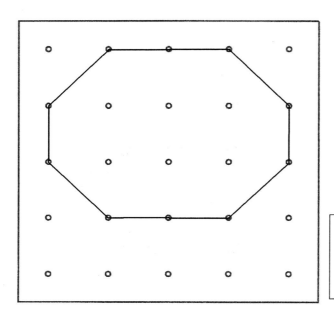

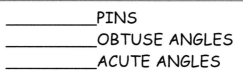

_____PINS
_____OBTUSE ANGLES
_____ACUTE ANGLES

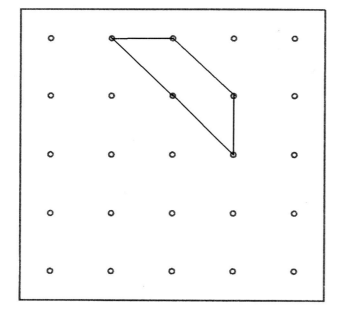

_____PINS
_____OBTUSE ANGLES
_____ACUTE ANGLES

GEO STAR CHART FOUR

On Planet Geo, some constellations in the night sky look like they overlap.

- Copy these constellations on your geoboard.
- Use <u>two</u> geobands to make them.
- Count the number of pins that each shape touches.
- Add the numbers together to find the sum.

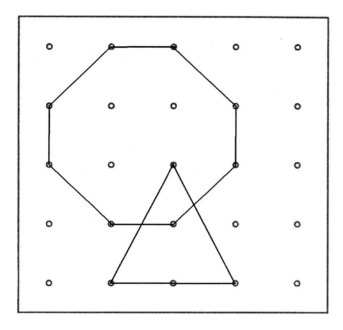

⬡ TOUCHES _____ PINS.

△ TOUCHES _____ PINS.

BOTH SHAPES TOUCH

_____ PINS.

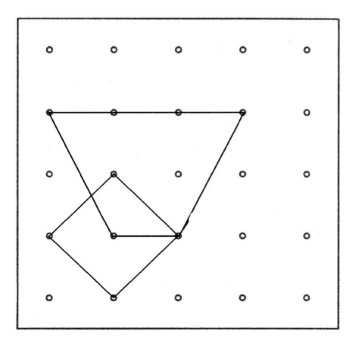

⬢ TOUCHES _____ PINS.

◇ TOUCHES _____ PINS.

BOTH SHAPES TOUCH
_____ PINS.

BE CAREFUL! If both shapes <u>share</u> a pin, you may only count it <u>once</u>.

GEO STAR CHART FIVE- INFINITY CHALLENGE

Chart your way home. Look carefully in the night sky with the alien's powerful telescope. *You might be able to spot earth!* It is right between two overlapping, triangle-shaped constellations.

Try this infinity challenge!
- **Use the clues to make the mystery shapes.**
- **Use two geobands and your geoboard.**

The first triangle has **2,2** and **4,2** as corner points. The third corner point is star **Zeo**, at points **3,5**. This is drawn for you below. Copy it on your geoboard.

You must add a second triangle to this picture. First, find two of its corner points at **4,4** and **4,2**. Connect these points on your geoboard with a rubber band. Then draw them on the geoboard at the left.

Now find the third star of this second triangle. It is at **1,4**. Stretch your geoboard rubber band to this point.

Now draw two more lines that complete the three sides of this triangle.

When these Star Charts are correctly drawn, a small speck will appear in the center. **Mark this with an "X." YOU HAVE FOUND EARTH!**

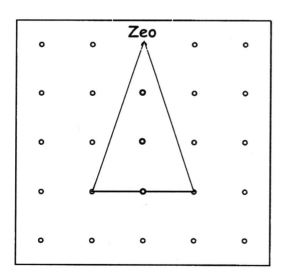

Zeo

Geoboard Dot Paper

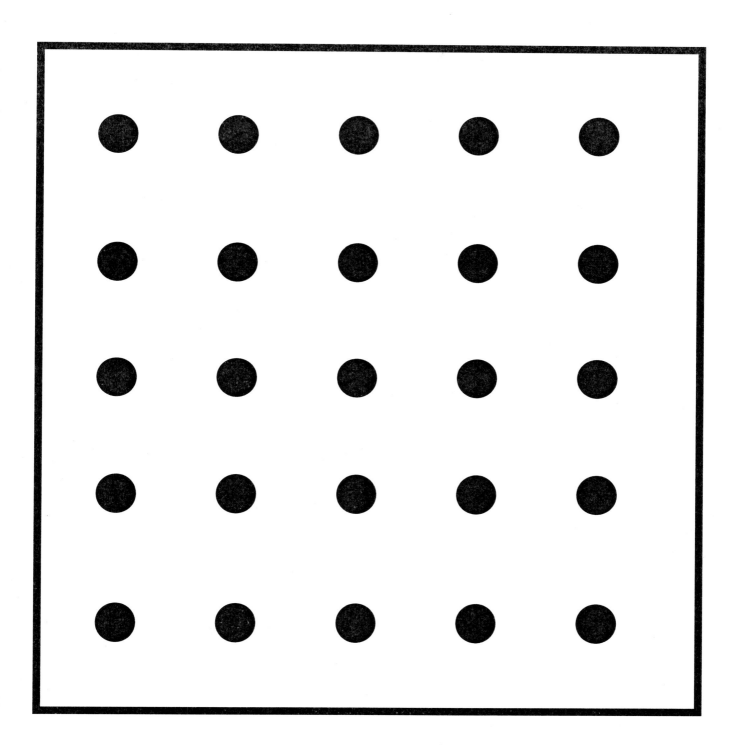

The Grande Finale

You made it back home safely! What a great astronaut you are! Did you know that someone named Goldie Locks also had some friends who were talking shapes? Read this whole contract before you begin. Be sure you read the score sheet on the last page too.

1. _____ Read the book called *Goldie Locks and the Three Squares*. Find out what was in the Three Square's house. Draw a picture of what you might find in <u>one</u> of the rooms of the Three Square's house. Use a plain sheet of white paper.

2. _____ Now, think back about your Planet Geo adventure. What if you had gone inside an alien's house on Planet Geo? Think about what you would you have seen.

© 2003 Pieces of Learning

- Design the outside of the alien's house on your geoboard. Use <u>one</u> rubber band.
- Copy this design to the **geoboard dot paper**. Use a ruler to make your lines straight.
- This house touches _____pins.
- It has _____ right angles, _____obtuse angles, and _____acute angles.

3. _____ Next, on a piece of construction paper, copy this same shape of your alien's house. Use a ruler to make straight lines.
   - Label the rooms of your house and add different-shaped furniture.
   - Show the shape of the food on the table, the chairs the aliens sit on and the beds that they sleep in. (Don't forget, Geo is a planet of shapes! Goldie Locks also found many shapes in the Three Square's House.)

4. _____ Write a paragraph on notebook paper explain-ing everything in your alien's house. Remember to use the *Geolanguage* you learned in Geofinity to describe the shapes you see in the different rooms.

5. _____ When you are finished, fill out the Grande Finale Score Card that is stapled to the back of your Grande Finale instructions.

Grande Finale Score Card

NAME _____

Score	Work That I Did
5	**Fantastic!** Both of the pictures that I drew have a lot of <u>detail</u>. I used lots of different shapes in my pictures and I followed the directions very well. I made a picture of a room in the Three Square's House and a picture of my alien's house on Planet Geo. The paragraph that I wrote is great! I used "Geolanguage" to describe the shapes in all of the rooms of my alien's house. I used details in my writing and wrote 5-7 sentences. I corrected my spelling.
4	**Very Good Job!** I did a very good job on both of my pictures. I used some shapes in them, and I followed the directions. My paragraph describes some of the shapes I found in the alien house. I used "Geolanguage" to describe these shapes and I wrote more than 4 sentences. I corrected my spelling.
3	**Good** My pictures and paragraph are average and have some detail. I followed the directions.
2	**O. K.** I drew the two pictures, and I wrote the paragraph, but I could have put in a little more detail.
1	I tried to do the Grande Finale, but I did not finish or follow directions. I left out some details and did not do my best.

What score do you think you should get (5, 4, 3, 2, or 1)?

_____

Why?

For the teacher: What score do you think the student should get on the Grande Finale? _____

Comments:

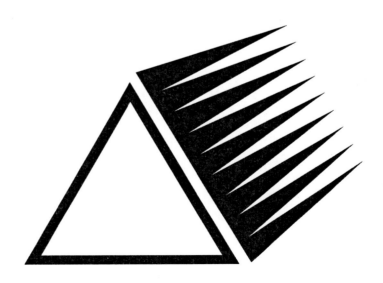

GEOFINITY
LEVEL 2
Contract

Name _____

Date _____

In a mysterious galaxy far away, there are planets shaped like polygons and aliens with bodies made of angles. This galaxy is called Infinity Landing. Are you ready for a visit?

In this Contract Unit you will study about geometric figures and different ways to measure them. You will also read and write about geometric shapes as you travel within the galaxy of Infinity Landing.

1. _____ Before blasting off for your destination in the galaxy, you will need to create a **Dictionary of Spatial Terms** to help you navigate. (Look in the Geofinity box for a folder by this title.)

2. _____ Now that you are a "Geo Whiz," Astronaut Al, your captain, needs you to inspect the ship before take-off. Complete the **Ship Shape activity**. (Look in the Geofinity box for a folder by this title.)

3. _____ Astronaut Al says you were out of this world! You are now ready for take-off. Astronaut Al wants you to study the flight patterns of his last class of students. His

students learned all about **Parallel and Perpendicular Lines** when they were flying. (Look in the Geofinity box for a folder by this title.)

4. _____ Now that your flight pattern is on an even course, you can head toward the **Polygon Planets** in this strange, new galaxy. Some are coming into view right now. (Look in the Geofinity box for a folder by this title.)

5. _____ Astronaut Al asks you to come to his Geo-class on the spaceship.
   • He says that it is very important for you to learn about angles and shapes so you can use them when you describe any structures you find on a planet where you land.
   • Using a geoboard and rubber bands from your classroom, complete the **Geoclass Packet**. (Look in the Geofinity box for a folder by this title.)

6. _____ You are moving very close to one of the Polygon Planets and have entered its gravitational field. It is time to land now on Planet Nonagon!
   • After a fairly smooth landing, you open the spaceship door and see an amazing sight. It looks like the ruins of a civilization. The ground floors of some old buildings are straight ahead!
   • You need to report to Earth and describe the **Perimeter** of each of these buildings. It is time to get to work. (Look in the Geofinity box for a folder by this title.)

7. _____ Look up ahead! Some aliens are approaching in the distance. The aliens appear to be made up of angles! Their space vehicles have angles, too! Get out your super telescope and **Scope Out Some Angles!** (Look in the Geofinity box for a folder by this title.)

8. _____ Grand Finale
   Well, you have to go home now. You have learned a lot about shapes, lines, angles, and perimeter. On the long trip home, you need to show Astronaut Al how much you have learned! Complete the **Grande Finale** using *The Greedy Triangle*. (Look in the Geofinity box, and find the directions for this activity and the book by this name.)

National Standards*
In Geofinity Level One and Level Two
the student will . . .

GEOMETRY
- Analyze characteristics and properties of two- and three-dimensional geometric shapes and develop mathematical arguments about geometric relationships.
- Specify locations and describe spatial relationships using coordinate geometry and other representational systems.
- Apply transformations and use symmetry to analyze mathematical situations.
- Use visualization, spatial reasoning, and modeling to solve problems.

MEASUREMENT
- Understand measurable attributes of objects and the units, systems, and processes of measurement.
- Apply appropriate techniques, tools, and formulas to determine measurements.

PROBLEM SOLVING
- Build new mathematical knowledge through problem solving.
- Solve problems that arise in mathematics and other contexts.
- Apply and adapt a variety of strategies to solve problems.
- Monitor and reflect on the process of mathematical problem solving.

CONNECTIONS
- Recognize and use connections among mathematical ideas.
- Understand how mathematical ideas interconnect and build on one another to produce a coherent whole.
- Recognize and apply mathematics in contexts outside of mathematics.

* From Principles and Standards for School Mathematics, Chapter 5, "Standards for Grades 3-5" http://standards.nctm.org

Dictionary of Spatial Terms

Follow these directions to make your own set of Picture Dictionary Flash Cards or a Dictionary Booklet.

1. Gather the following materials:

   - 15 3" x 5" index cards or paper to make a booklet
   - Glue, scissors, pencil, markers, or crayons
   - Definition sheet (found in Geofinity box)
   - Ruler

2. Cut out the definitions on the Definitions in Geometry sheet.

3. On one side of each index card (or booklet page) paste a definition. On the other side of the card or page draw an illustration of the definition. Complete one card or page for each definition listed. Be sure and use your ruler!

Definitions in Geometry

Right Angle
An angle that is formed when two lines meet and form an "L." This angle is 90 degrees.

Acute Angle
An angle that is less than a right angle. This angle is less than 90 degrees.

Obtuse Angle
An angle that is bigger than a right angle. The angle formed is greater than 90 degrees.

Quadrilateral
A figure with four sides and four angles.

Perpendicular Lines
Two lines that intersect and form right angles.

Polygon
A closed figure made of line segments.

Parallel Lines
Lines that move out in the same direction and are always the same distance apart. These lines never meet.

Parallelogram
A figure having four sides, with the opposite sides parallel and of equal length.

Definitions in Geometry

Triangle
A polygon with three sides.

Square
A quadrilateral with
four equal sides and
four right angles.

Rectangle
A parallelogram with
four right angles.

Trapezoid
A quadrilateral with
only one pair
of parallel sides.

Pentagon
A five-sided polygon with
five inside angles.

Hexagon
A six-sided polygon with
six inside angles.

Octagon
An eight-sided polygon with
eight inside angles.

Nonagon
A nine-sided polygon with
nine inside angles.

Ship Shape

Study the rocket ship. Use the key and help
Astronaut Al make sure that all of your gear is on board
and ready for Blast-Off!!

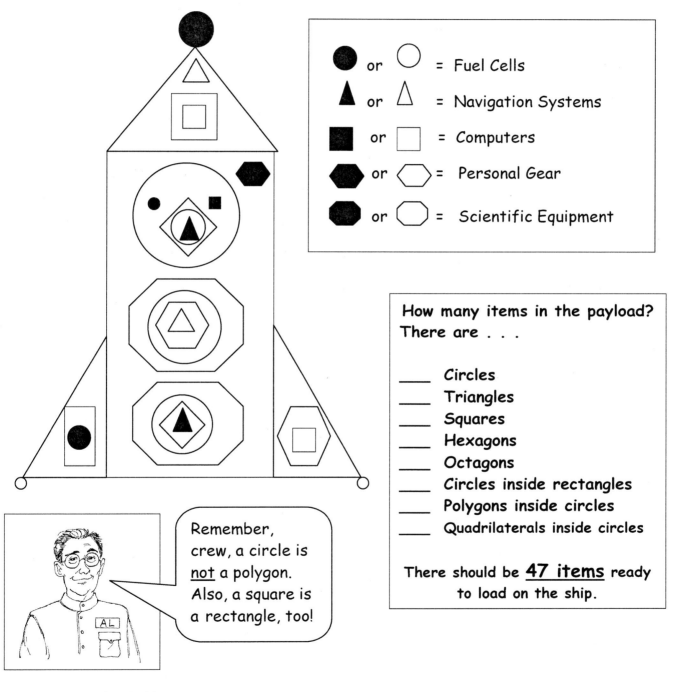

Remember,
crew, a circle is
<u>not</u> a polygon.
Also, a square is
a rectangle, too!

**How many items in the payload?
There are . . .**

____ Circles
____ Triangles
____ Squares
____ Hexagons
____ Octagons
____ Circles inside rectangles
____ Polygons inside circles
____ Quadrilaterals inside circles

There should be **47 items** ready
to load on the ship.

Crew Member's Name: _____

Parallel and Perpendicular Lines

Astronaut Al wants you to look at some flight patterns from his last class of students. When flying this spaceship, you will learn about two flight plans: <u>Parallel</u> and <u>Perpendicular</u>. These words will help you know which way to steer your spaceship.

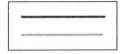

These two straight paths are parallel because they never cross and always stay the same distance apart. If your ship's path always stays parallel to another ship, you will not crash into each other. Your paths will never meet.

These line segments are perpendicular. They cross or meet to form a square corner. (90 degrees)

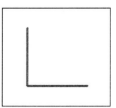

If you fly your ship perpendicular to another ship, you may find yourself crashing into it during your trip. Your paths will meet.

Look at the flight paths to the right.
They are: (circle one)

Parallel   Perpendicular

48   © 2003 Pieces of Learning

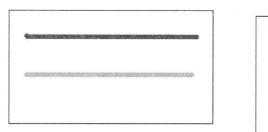

These two flight paths are:
(circle one)

Parallel   Perpendicular

Are these flight paths parallel, perpendicular, or neither?
(Print the answer under the flight path.)

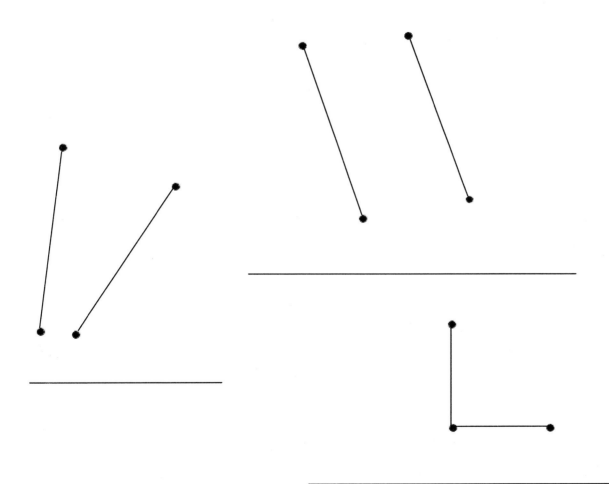

Polygon Planets

Name _____

The Polygon planets in the mysterious galaxy of Infinity Landing are made up of very special shapes.

- Polygons are flat, closed shapes with three or more sides. All of the sides must be straight.
- Four-sided polygons are called quadrilaterals.
- You will learn the names of some of the quadrilaterals.

The Polygon planets coming into your view contain shapes that look like these.

Parallelogram

A figure having four sides, with the opposite sides parallel and of equal length.

Rectangle

A parallelogram with four right angles

Square

A quadrilateral with four equal sides and four right angles.

Trapezoid

A quadrilateral with only one pair of parallel sides.

Polygon Planet Nonagon

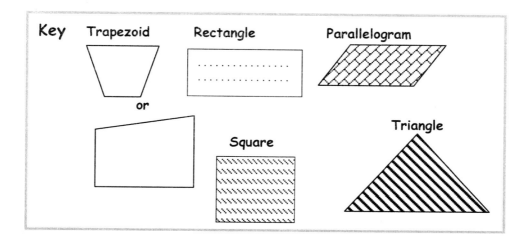

Color key Polygon Planet Nonagon to show your friends on Earth. First, look at the polygons in the key above. Choose a different color for each kind of shape, and color the shapes in the key.

Now color in Polygon Planet Nonagon using the same colors as your key. Be careful! Triangles, trapezoids, squares and parallelograms come in different shapes and sizes.

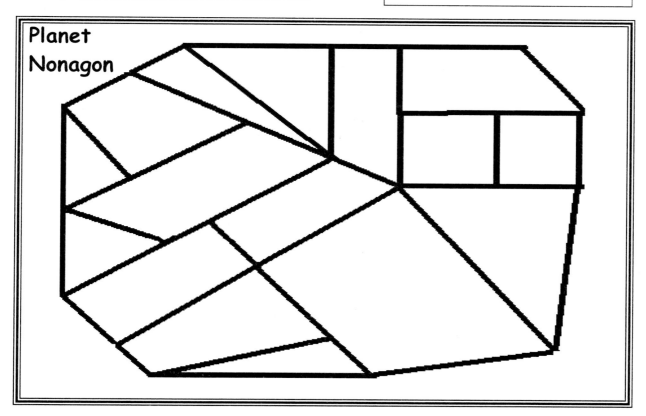

GEOCLASS

PACKET

GEOCLASS
Assignment 1

- Copy each shape on your geoboard and recording sheet.
- Find each <u>right angle</u>, and mark it with an **X** on your recording sheet.

1.

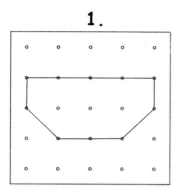

2.

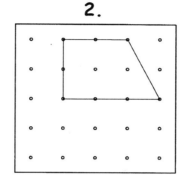

3.

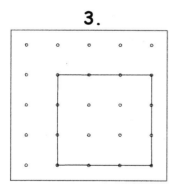

4.

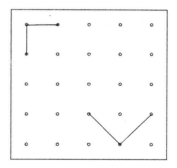

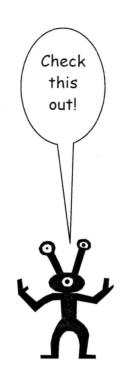

These are Right angles

5. Bonus Problem

Now try a real challenge! Make a shape that has **four sides** and **only one right angle.** First try it on your geoboard, then on your recording sheet. Mark the right angle with an **X**.

Assignment 1
RECORDING SHEET

1.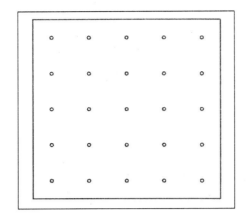

2.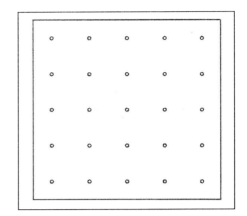

3.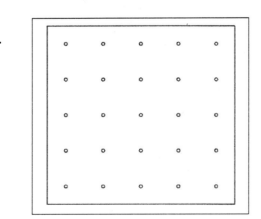

4.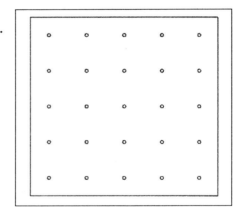

5.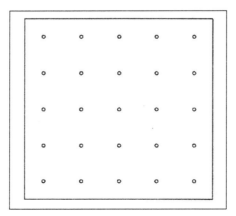

GEOCLASS

Assignment 2

- Copy each shape on your geoboard.
- Copy again on your recording sheet.
- Find each angle that is LESS than a right angle, and mark with an **X** on your recording sheet.
- This is called an <u>ACUTE</u> angle.

1

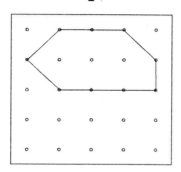

2

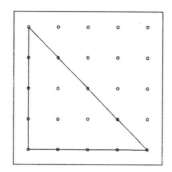

3

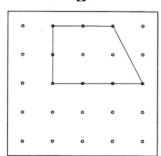

Right angles

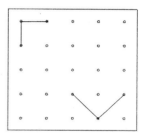

Less than right angles (acute)

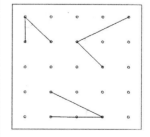

4. Bonus Problem

Try this challenge! Make a shape that has **three sides** with **one right angle** and **two acute angles**. First make it on your geoboard, and then on your recording sheet.

Assignment 2
RECORDING SHEET

1.

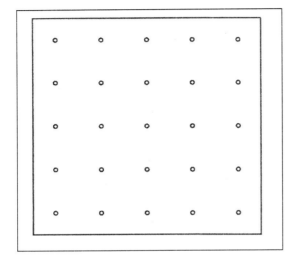

2.

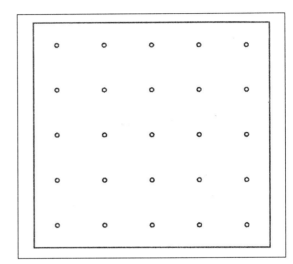

3.

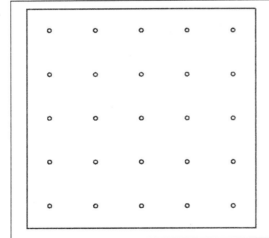

4.

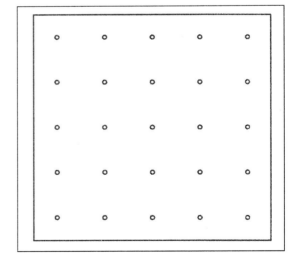

GEOCLASS
Assignment 3

- Copy each shape on your geoboard.
- Copy again on your recording sheet.
- Find each angle that is GREATER than a right angle, and mark with an **X** on your recording sheet.
- This is called an <u>OBTUSE</u> angle.

Check this out!

1

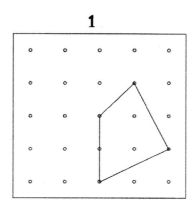

2

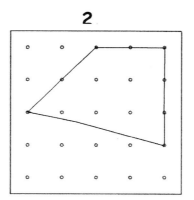

Right angles

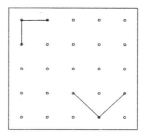

3

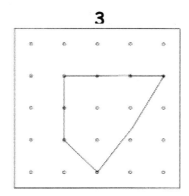

Greater than right angles

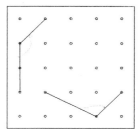

---

4. Bonus Problem

Make a shape that has **five sides and at least one angle greater than a right angle.** Make it on your Geoboard first, then on your recording sheet.

Assignment 3
RECORDING SHEET

1.
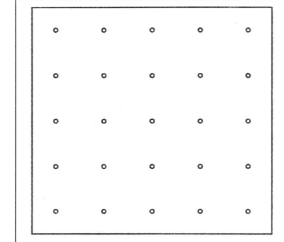

2.

3.
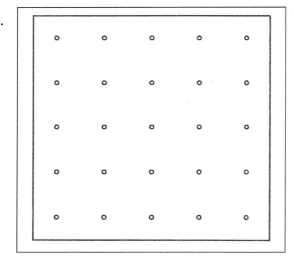

4.

GEOCLASS
Assignment 4

- Copy each shape on your geoboard.
- Copy again on your recording sheet.
- Find each 90-degree angle and mark it with an **X** on your recording sheet.

1. 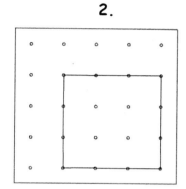   **2.**

Right angles are 90 degrees.

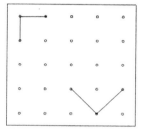

Bonus Problems

3. Make a shape that has **five sides**, and **two 90-degree angles**.

4. Make a shape that has **eight sides**, and **no 90-degree angles**.

Assignment 4
RECORDING SHEET

1.
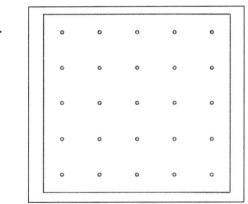

2.
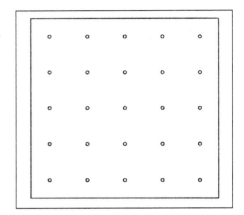

3.
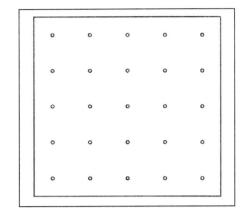

4.
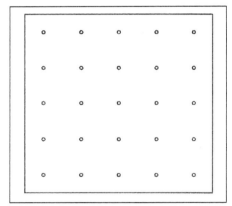

GEOCLASS
Assignment 5

- Copy each shape on your geoboard and recording sheet.
- Find each angle that is LESS than a 90-degree angle and mark it with an **X** on your recording sheet.

1.

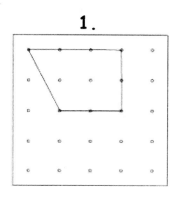

2.

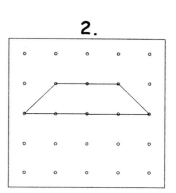

3.

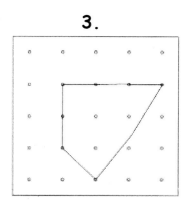

4.

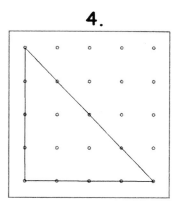

These are . . .

90 degree angles

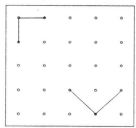

These are

Less than 90 degree angles

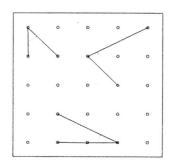

5. Bonus Problem
Make a shape that has **four sides**, and **two angles less than 90 degrees**.

Assignment 5
RECORDING SHEET

1.
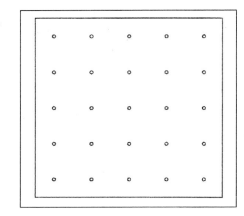

2.
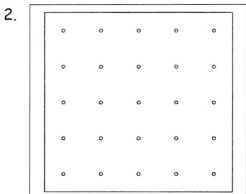

3.
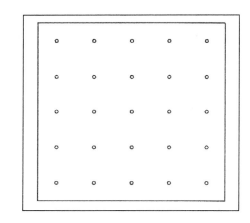

4.
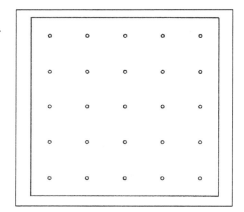

5.
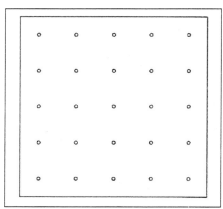

An Alien Civilization  PERIMETER

You have uncovered an ancient alien civilization! All that is left are the outlines of ancient homes, market-places, and other buildings. You must report back to your world about this incredible find by copying each building on your geoboard and then accurately recording the sizes of each building.

The opera hall is really one large and one small rectangle put together.

EXAMPLE: Opera Hall

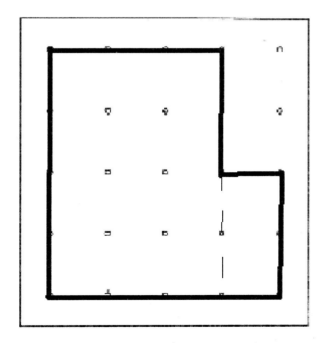

Distance around the large rectangle is <u>14</u> units.

Distance around the small rectangle is <u>6</u> units.

Total distance around the ancient opera hall is <u>16</u> units.

Now try this new building!

A Small Temple

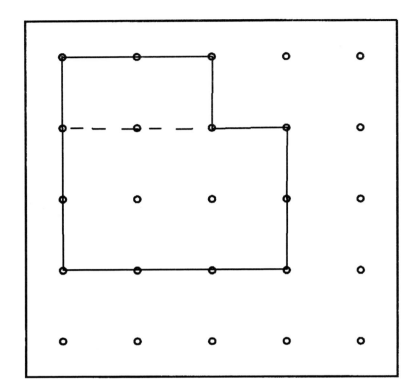

Distance around the big rectangle is _____ units.

Distance around the small rectangle is _____ units.

Distance around entire temple is _____ units.

Well Done, Astronaut! In the distance you spot three more building sites. You need to find the **perimeter** of each so you can report these findings back to Earth, too.

Wealthy Man's Home

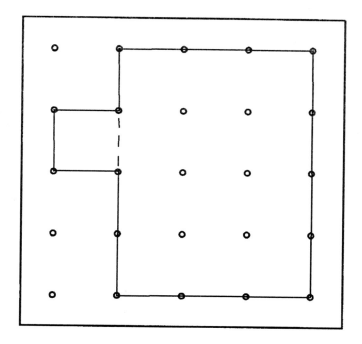

Distance around the big rectangle is _____ units.

Distance around the small square is _____ units.

Distance around the home is _____ units.

Small Food Stall

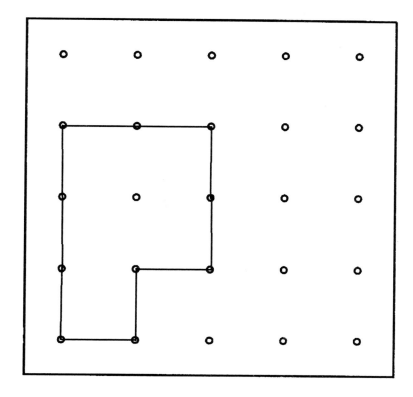

Distance around the big rectangle is _____ units.

Distance around the small square is _____ units.

Distance around the food stall is _____ units.

Leather Craftsman's Shop

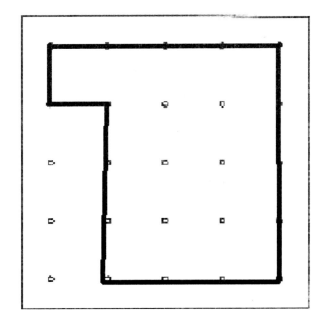

Distance around the big rectangle is _____ units.

Distance around the small square is _____ units.

Distance around the leather craftsman's shop is _____ units.

People on Earth will also need to know about some special building sites you found that had three special shapes on the inside.

The three special shapes are:

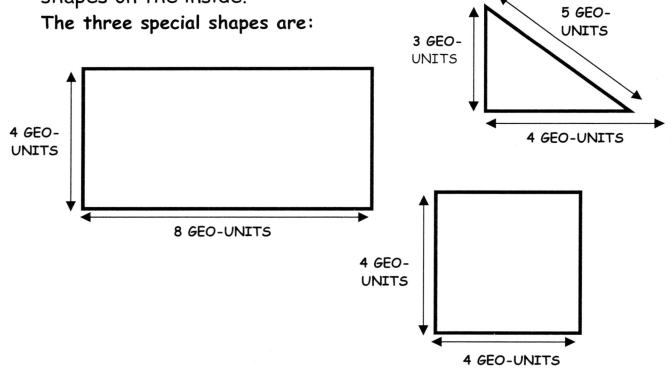

Astronaut Al says that these special buildings were probably called temples. Here are the three temples. They were made from the same three shapes but arranged in different ways. See if you can figure out the perimeter of these three unique buildings.

ANCIENT TEMPLE 1
PERIMETER IS
_____ GEO-UNITS.

ANCIENT TEMPLE 2
PERIMETER IS _____ GEO-UNITS.

ANCIENT TEMPLE 3
IS _____ GEO-UNITS.

Scope Out Some Angles

NAME _____

DATE _____

Are the angles in the pictures right angles, acute angles, or obtuse angles? Label: **R, A, or O.**

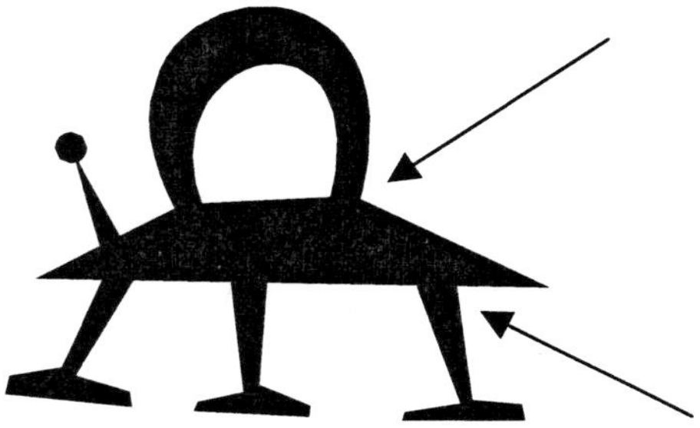

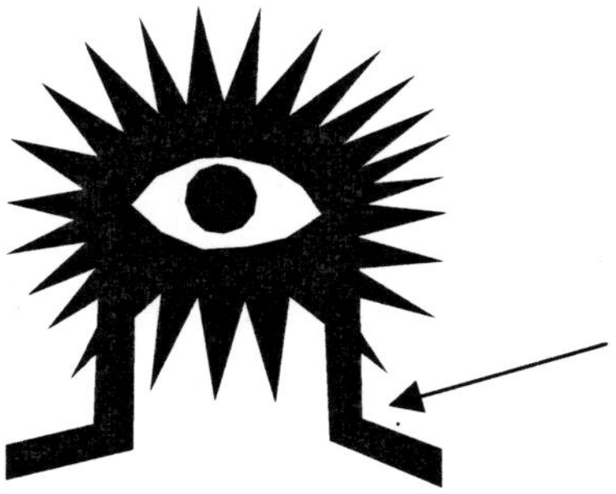

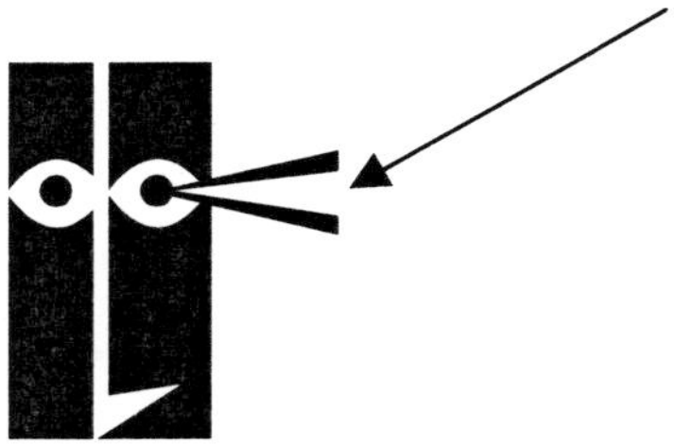

Are there more obtuse angles or acute angles? _____

The Greedy Triangle

THE GRANDE FINALE

NAME _____

1. _____ Read the book in the Geofinity box called *The Greedy Triangle* by Marilyn Burns. Think about how the little triangle changed from one shape to another.

2. _____ Now take a geoboard, and using ONE large rubber band, make a shape just like one of the buildings you saw on Planet Nonagon. Keep this shape on your geoboard for now.

3. _____ Take some geoboard dot paper. Use this paper and a pencil to create the same shape. Label this drawing with the title <u>Planet Nonagon Building.</u>

4. Figure out the perimeter for this building.
   What is it? _____
   (answer)

5. How many right angles does it have? _____

6. How many acute angles does it have? _____

7. How many obtuse angles does it have? _____

8. Now change the building shape (just like the Greedy Triangle did). Make this new shape on your geoboard with the rubber bands. Make it interesting. Sketch it on a new piece of geoboard dot paper, and give it a title that says "New Building on Planet Nonagon.

   ▪ How many right angles does it have? _____

   ▪ How many acute angles? _____

   ▪ How many obtuse angles does the new building have? _____

   ▪ What is the perimeter of the new building? _____

9. Think about this new building shape and <u>how</u> the ancient aliens on Planet Nonagon would have used it.

   • _____ *Plan* a short story about a day with the aliens in this new building. What does the building look like inside? What is happening in each of the rooms? What are the aliens doing inside?

- _____ Make sure your story plan has a beginning, middle, and end. *Show* your plans, story map, or outline to your teacher.

- _____ *Write* the short story about this building and the ancient aliens. Add lots of details! Use the computer if one is available. If not, use paper and pencil.

- _____ Include at least *one picture* of the ancient aliens *inside or outside this building*.

- _____ Edit the final draft of your story for spelling and punctuation.

10. _____ When you are finished, complete the Grande Finale checklist on the next page.

Good job!
I hope you join me on another adventure sometime soon.
Welcome Home!

AL

The Grande Finale Check List

NAME _____

First, answer these questions with a **YES** or **NO**.

1. Did you read the book called *The Greedy Triangle* by Marilyn Burns? _____

2. Did you take geoboard dot paper and create a shape with the title "Planet Nonagon Building"? _____

3. Did you figure out the perimeter, right angles, and obtuse angles of the planet Nonagon building? _____

4. Did you make the "New Building on Planet Nonagon" on your geoboard dot paper? _____

5. Did you figure out the angles and perimeter of the new building? _____

6. Did you write a short story and include a picture about what the ancient aliens would have done in your building? _____

If you answered **NO** to any of these questions, please go back and complete the missing assignments.

What score do you think you should get on the Greedy Triangle Grande Finale?

SCORE	WHAT I DID
5	I did a <u>fantastic</u> job on all of this. I followed directions, made the buildings, and added detail to my work. I wrote a story about the ancient aliens and what took place in their building. My story has a beginning, middle, and end. My spelling and punctuation are excellent. I included a detailed picture.
4	I did a <u>very good</u> job on my buildings. I wrote a very good story that included details about my ancient alien building and what took place there. My story has a beginning, middle, and end. I think my spelling and punctuation are very good. I made a nice picture of the alien building.
3	I did a <u>good</u> job on my buildings, my story, and my picture. I remembered to put periods at the end of my sentences. I think my words are spelled correctly. I made a picture.
2	My buildings, story, and my pictures are <u>O.K.</u> I am not sure if I have a good beginning, middle, and end to my story. I think I also have some problems with spelling or periods in my sentences. I made a picture of the alien building.
1	I think I did not do my best and did not follow all of the directions.

Student: What score do you think you should get? _____

Why?

Teacher: What score do you think the student should get on the Grande Finale? ____

Comments:

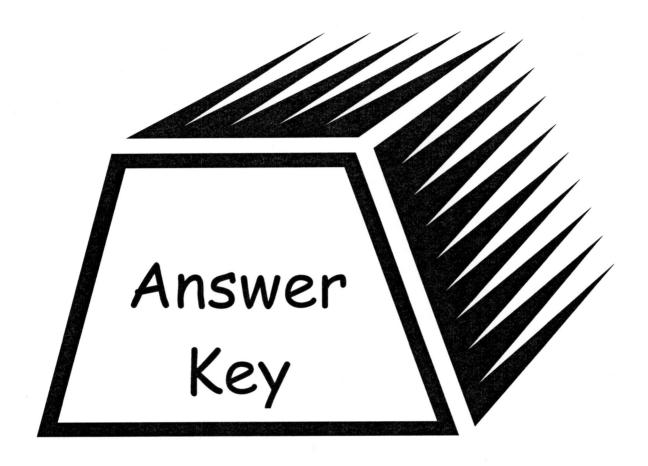

Angle School

The aliens insist that you know your angles. Look at these polygons. Do you see any angles? Place an **X** on each angle you see.

1. X   X
    X   X

2.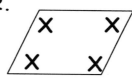
    X X
    X X

3. X
    X   X

4. X X
    X   X
    X X

5.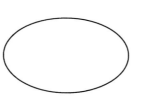

6. X   X
    X   X
    X

Now find the right angles. Place an X on each right angle!

7.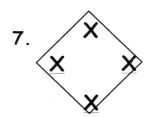

8.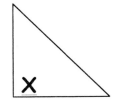

9.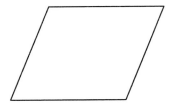

Now find the acute angles. Place an X on each acute angle!

10.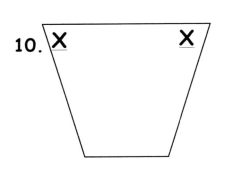

11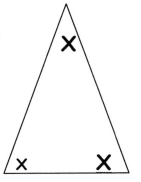

12.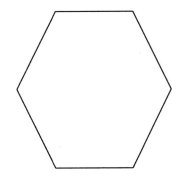

Finally, find the obtuse angles. Place an X on each obtuse angle.

13.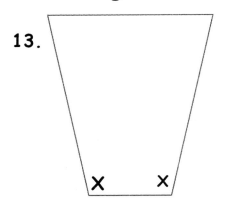

14.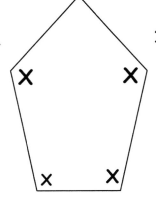

15.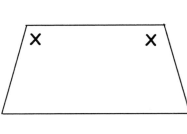

STAR CHARTS
FIND THE PLANETS

Page 30

Page 30

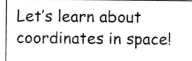

Let's learn about coordinates in space!

You have gone on a field trip to the observatory. Here you will learn Planet Geo Navigation and make a star chart to get you home.

- Look at the Geo Star Chart below.
- Each planet is marked with a square, a diamond, an octagon, or a star.
- Find the location by telling how many places it is from the left side and the bottom. These locations are your planet coordinates.

GEO STAR CHART ONE

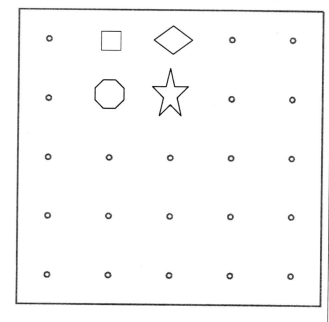

PLANET ☐ IS _2__ FROM THE LEFT SIDE AND _5___ FROM THE BOTTOM OF THE GRID.

PLANET ◇ IS _3___ FROM THE LEFT AND___5_ FROM THE BOTTOM OF THE GRID.

PLANET ⬡ IS _2___ FROM THE LEFT AND_4___ FROM THE BOTTOM OF THE GRID.

PLANET ☆ IS _3___ FROM THE LEFT AND_4___ FROM THE BOTTOM OF THE GRID.

GEO STAR CHART TWO

Now practice making Star Charts on your geoboard. Make each constellation in the correct location on your geoboard. Count the total number of pins the rubber band touches.

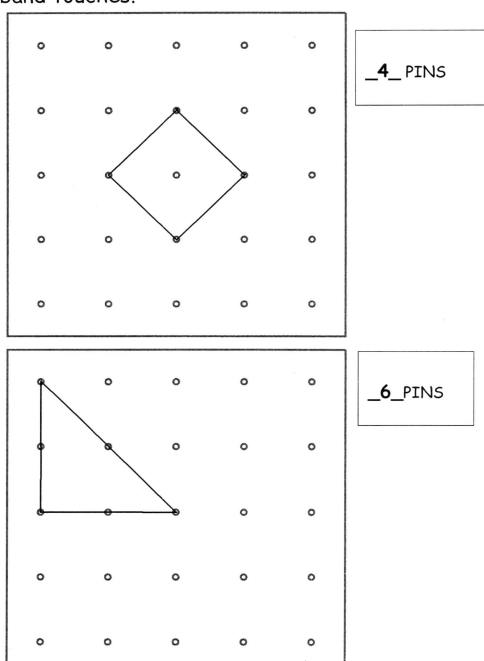

_4_ PINS

_6_PINS

GEO STAR CHART THREE

Make each constellation on your geoboard.
Count the total number of pins the rubber
band touches. Put an "**X**" on <u>each</u> acute angle
in the figures below.

You may use your
Geolanguage
Guide book for
help.

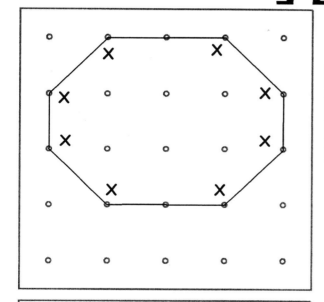

> __10____ PINS
> __ 8____ OBTUSE ANGLES
> __ 0____ ACUTE ANGLES

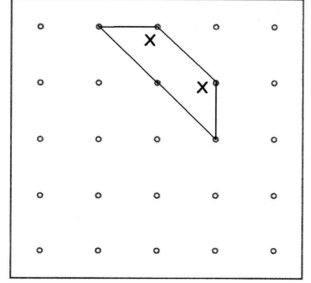

> __5__ PINS
> __2__ OBTUSE ANGLES
> __2__ ACUTE ANGLES

GEO STAR CHART FOUR

Page 33

On planet geo, some constellations in the night sky look like they overlap.

- Copy these constellations on your geoboard.
- Use two geobands to make them.
- Count the number of pins each shape touches.
- Add them together to find the sum.

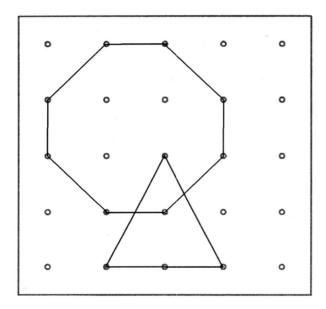

⬡ TOUCHES __8__ PINS.

△ TOUCHES __4__ PINS.

BOTH SHAPES TOUCH __12__ PINS.

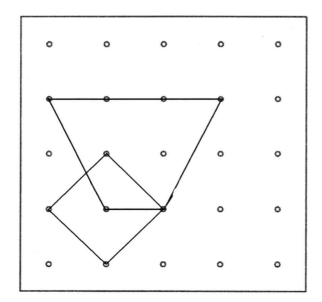

▽ TOUCHES __6__ PINS.

◇ TOUCHES __4__ PINS.

BOTH SHAPES TOUCH __9__ PINS.

BE CAREFUL! If both shapes share a pin, you may only count it once.

GEO STAR CHART FIVE
INFINITY CHALLENGE

CHART YOUR WAY HOME

Look carefully in the night sky with the aliens' powerful telescope. *You might be able to spot Earth!* It is right between two overlapping, triangle-shaped constellations.

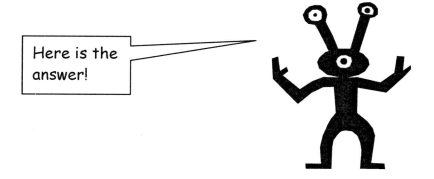

Here is the answer!

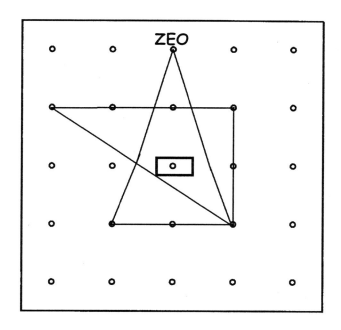

ZEO

Ship Shape

Study the rocket ship. Use the key and help Astronaut Al make sure that all of your gear is on board and ready for Blast-Off!!

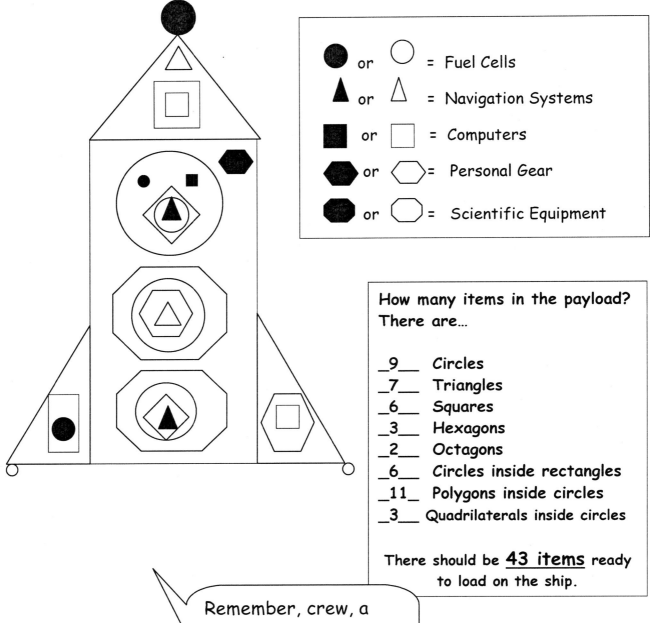

or ⬤ or ◯ = Fuel Cells

▲ or △ = Navigation Systems

◼ or ☐ = Computers

⬣ or ⬡ = Personal Gear

⬢ or ◯ = Scientific Equipment

How many items in the payload?
There are…

_9__   Circles
_7__   Triangles
_6__   Squares
_3__   Hexagons
_2__   Octagons
_6__   Circles inside rectangles
_11_   Polygons inside circles
_3__   Quadrilaterals inside circles

There should be **43 items** ready to load on the ship.

Remember, crew, a circle is <u>not</u> a polygon. Also, a square is a rectangle too!

Parallel and Perpendicular Lines

Astronaut Al wants you to look at some flight patterns from his last class of students. When flying this space ship, you will learn about two flight plans: <u>Parallel</u> or <u>Perpendicular</u>. These words will help you know which way to steer your space ship.

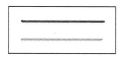

These two straight paths are parallel because they never cross and always stay the same distance apart. If your ship's path always stays parallel to another ship, you will not crash into each other. Your paths will not meet.

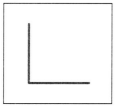

These line segments are perpendicular. They cross or meet to form a square corner. (90 degrees) If you fly your ship perpendicular to another ship, you may find yourself crashing into it during your trip. Your paths will meet.

These two flight paths are:

Parallel (Perpendicular)

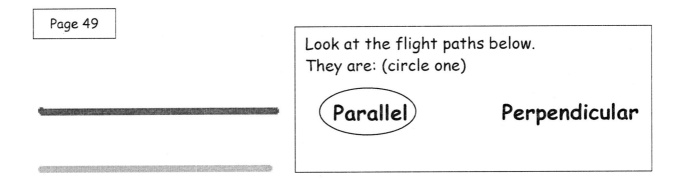

Look at the flight paths below.
They are: (circle one)

(Parallel)   Perpendicular

Are these flight paths parallel, perpendicular, or neither? (Print the answer under the flight path.)

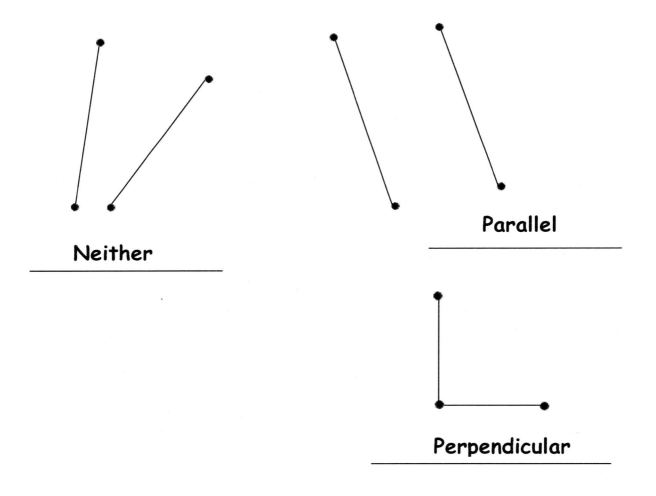

Neither
_____

Parallel
_____

Perpendicular
_____

POLYGON PLANETS

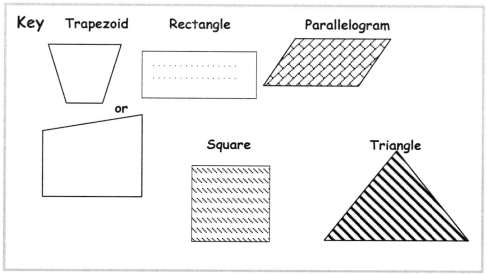

Note: Rectangles and squares are also parallelograms. If the student marks these as parallelograms, do not mark "incorrect." Encourage the student to ask "What else could this be?" A square is also a rectangle.

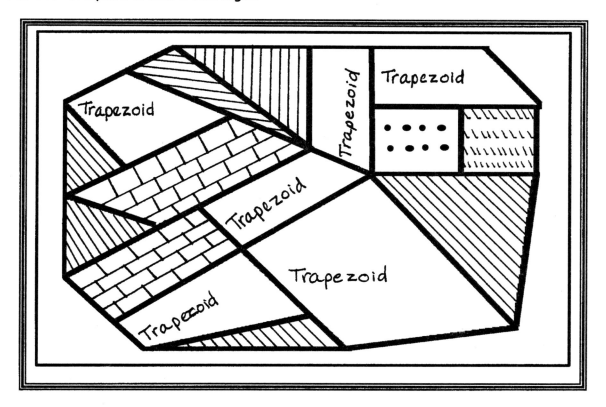

GEOCLASS

Assignment 1 Page 53

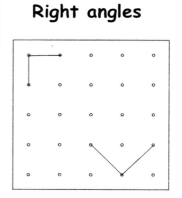

Check this out!

- Copy each shape on your geoboard and recording sheet.
- Find each right angle, and mark it with an **X** on your recording sheet.

1.

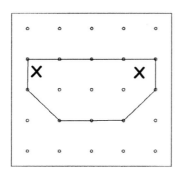

2.

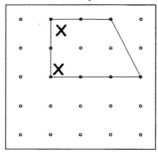

These are

Right angles

3.

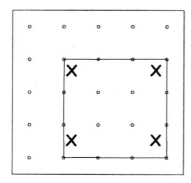

4.

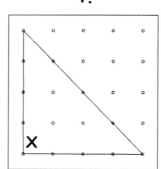

5. Bonus Problem

Now try a real challenge! Make a shape that has **four sides,** and **only one right angle.** First try it on your geoboard, then on your recording sheet. Mark the right angle with an **X.** This is one possible answer.

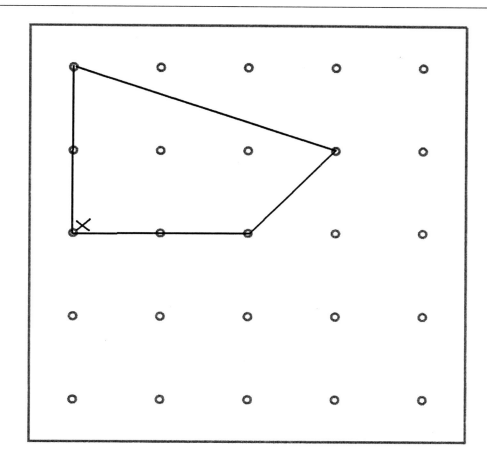

GEOCLASS

Assignment 2 Page 55

- Copy each shape on your geoboard.
- Copy again on your recording sheet.
- Find each angle that is LESS than a right angle, and mark with an **X** on your recording sheet. This is called an <u>ACUTE</u> angle.

Check this out!

1.

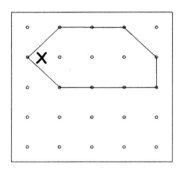

2.

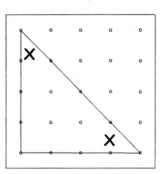

3.

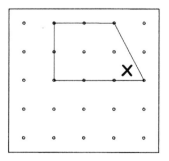

Right angles

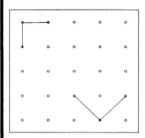

Less than right angles (acute)

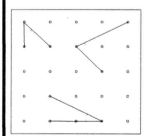

4. Bonus Problem

Try this challenge: **Make a shape that has three sides with one right angle and two acute angles.** First make it on your geoboard, and then on your recording sheet.

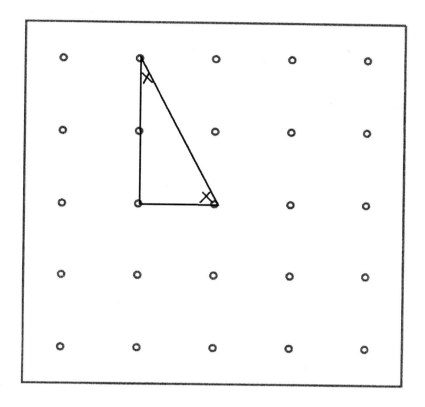

GEOCLASS

Assignment 3 Page 57

Check this out!

- Copy each shape on your geoboard.
- Copy again on your recording sheet.
- Find each angle that is GREATER than a right angle, and mark with an **X** on your recording sheet.
  This is called an <u>OBTUSE</u> angle.

1.

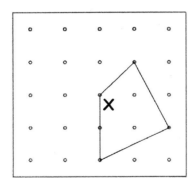

2.

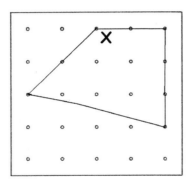

3.

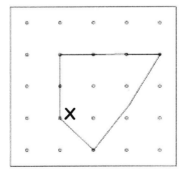

Right angles

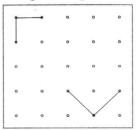

Greater than right angles (obtuse)

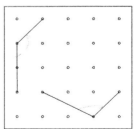

4. Bonus Problem

Make a shape that has five sides, and at least one angle greater than a right angle. Make it on your Geoboard first, then on your recording sheet. This is one possible answer.

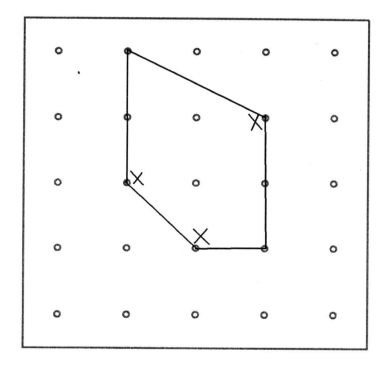

GEOCLASS

Assignment 4 Page 59

- Copy each shape on your geoboard.
- Copy again on your recording sheet.
- Find each 90-degree angle and mark it with an **X** on your recording sheet.

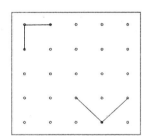

1.

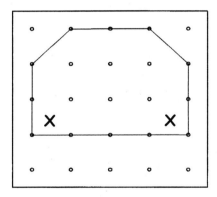

2.

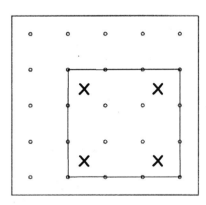

Right angles are 90 degrees. These are 90-degree angles.

Bonus Problems

3. Make a shape that has **five sides**, and two **90-degree angles**.

4. Make a shape that has **eight sides**, and no **90-degree angles**.

3.

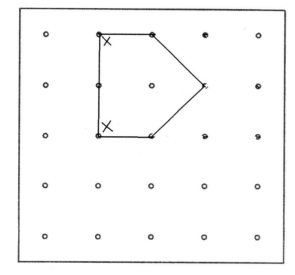

4.

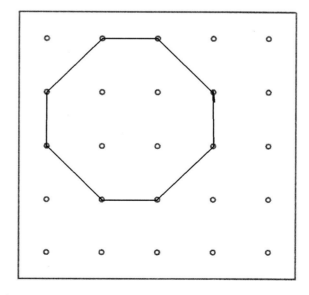

GEOCLASS

Assignment 5 Page 61

- Copy each shape on your geoboard and recording sheet.
- Find each angle that is LESS than a 90-degree angle and mark it with an **X** on your recording sheet.

1.

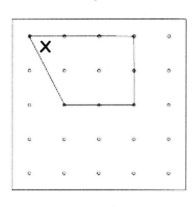

2.

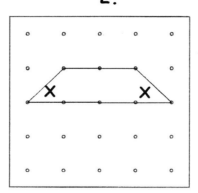

These are . . .

90-degree angles

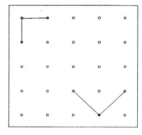

3.

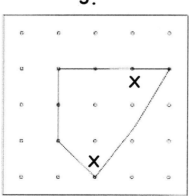

4.

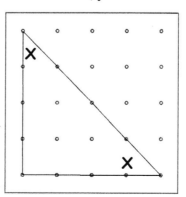

These are . . .

Less than 90-degree angles.

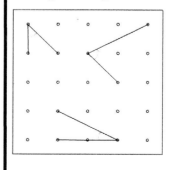

5. Bonus Problem

Make a shape that has four sides, and two angles less than 90 degrees. This is one possible solution. Answers will vary.

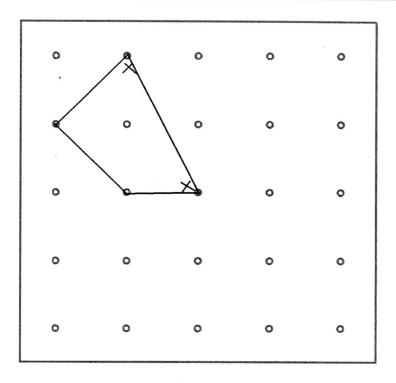

Perimeter: An Alien Civilization

Now try this new building!

A Small Temple

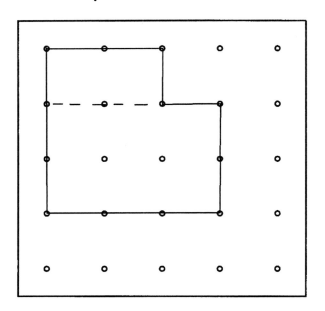

Distance around the big rectangle is **10** units.

Distance around the small rectangle is **6** units.

Distance around entire temple is **12** units.

Well Done, Astronaut! In the distance you spot three more building sites. You need to find the perimeter of each so you can report these findings back to Earth, too.

Wealthy Man's Home

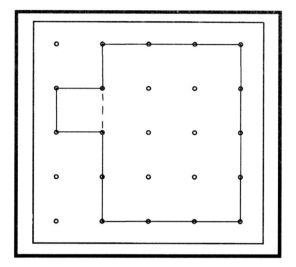

Distance around the big rectangle is **14** units.

Distance around the small square is **4** units.

Distance around the home is **16** units.

Small Food Stall

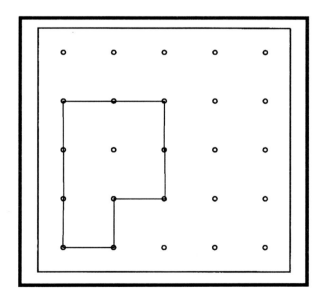

Distance around the big rectangle is **8** units.

Distance around the small square is **4** units.

Distance around the food stall is **10** units.

Leather Craftsman's Shop

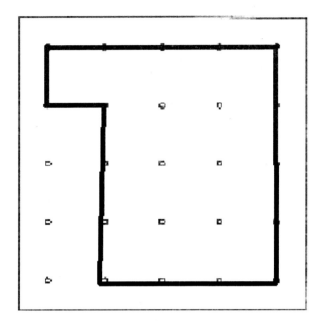

Distance around the big rectangle is **14** units.

Distance around the small square is **4** units.

Distance around the leather craftsman's shop is **16** units.

People on Earth will also need to know about some special building sites you found that had **three** special shapes on the inside. The three special shapes are:

4 GEO-UNITS

8 GEO-UNITS

3 GEO-UNITS

5 GEO-UNITS

4 GEO-UNITS

4 GEO-UNITS

4 GEO-UNITS

Astronaut Al says that these special buildings were probably called temples. Here are the three temples. They were made from the same three shapes but arranged in different ways. See if you can figure out the perimeter of these three unique buildings.

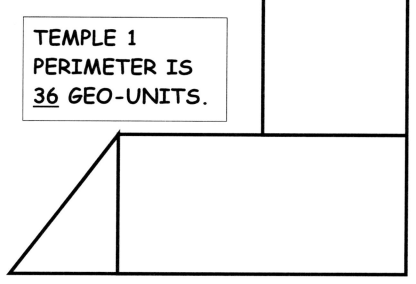

TEMPLE 1 PERIMETER IS <u>36</u> GEO-UNITS.

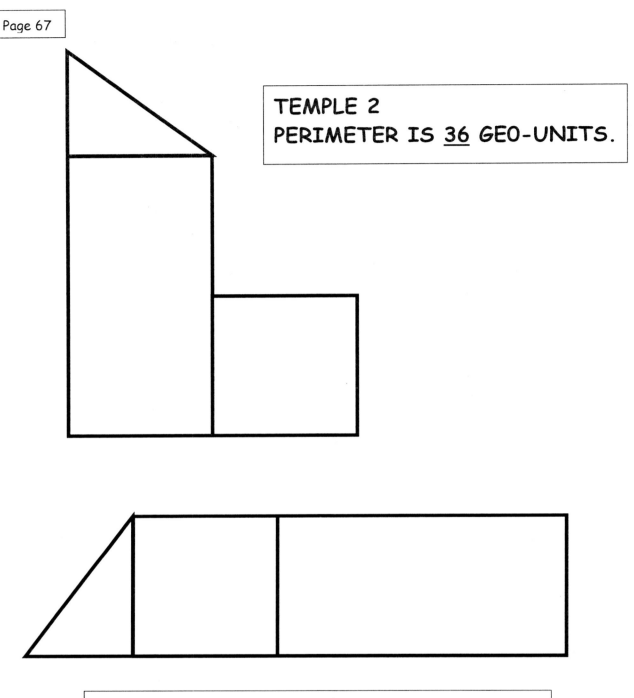

TEMPLE 2
PERIMETER IS <u>36</u> GEO-UNITS.

ANCIENT TEMPLE 3 IS <u>36</u> GEO-UNITS.

Scope Out Some Angles

NAME _____

DATE _____

Are the angles in the pictures right angles, acute angles, or obtuse angles? Label: **R, A,** or **O.**

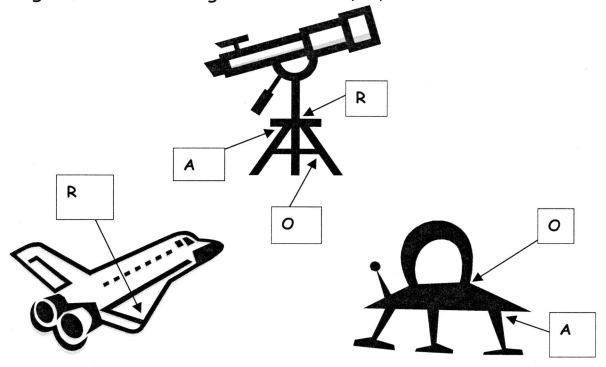

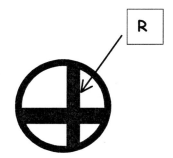

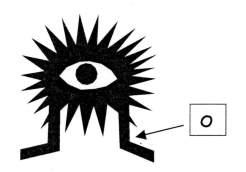

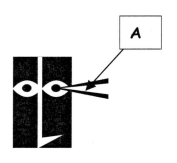

Are there more obtuse angles or acute angles? __OBTUSE_____

Geofinity